JUNIOR
BIOGRAPHY

ANCIENT
CIVILIZATIONS

MARCO
POLO

JOHN BANKSTON

Mitchell Lane
PUBLISHERS

P.O. Box 196
Hockessin, Delaware 19707
Visit us on the web: www.mitchelllane.com
Comments? Email us: mitchelllane@mitchelllane.com

JUNIOR
BIOGRAPHY
FROM
ANCIENT
CIVILIZATIONS

Alexander the Great • Archimedes
Augustus Caesar • Confucius • Genghis Khan
Homer • Leif Erikson • Marco Polo
Nero • Socrates

Copyright © 2014 by Mitchell Lane Publishers

Printing   1   2   3   4   5   6   7   8   9

ABOUT THE AUTHOR: Born in Boston, Massachusetts, John Bankston began writing articles while still a teenager. Since then, over two hundred of his articles have been published in magazines and newspapers across the country, including travel articles in *The Tallahassee Democrat*, *The Orlando Sentinel* and *The Tallahassean*. He is the author of over eighty books for young adults, including biographies of scientist Stephen Hawking, author F. Scott Fitzgerald, and actor Jodi Foster.

PUBLISHER'S NOTE: The facts on which the story in this book is based have been thoroughly researched. Documentation of such research can be found on pages 45-46. While every possible effort has been made to ensure accuracy, the publisher will not assume liability for damages caused by inaccuracies in the data, and makes no warranty on the accuracy of the information contained herein.

Library of Congress
Cataloging-in-Publication Data

Bankston, John.
 Marco Polo / by John Bankston.
   pages cm. — (Junior biography from ancient civilizations)
 Includes bibliographical references and index.
 ISBN 978-1-61228-434-7 (library bound)
 1. Polo, Marco, 1254-1323?—Travel—Juvenile literature. 2. Explorers—Italy—Biography—Juvenile literature. 3. Travel, Medieval—Juvenile literature. 4. Asia—Description and travel—Juvenile literature. I. Title.
 G370.P9.B275 2014
 910.92—dc23
 [B]
                                       2013012558

eBook ISBN: 9781612284965

                                            PLB

CONTENTS

Phonetic pronunciations of words in **bold**
can be found on page 47.

Marco Polo described visiting places few Europeans had ever seen before. Often called a liar during his lifetime, today he is a celebrated son of Italy. This mosaic at Villa Hanbury in Ventimiglia, Italy depicts an older Marco Polo, long after his travels had ended.

CHAPTER 1

The Description of the World

Marco Polo's father was a merchant named **Niccolò**,* who bought and sold jewels and silk. Marco's mother was pregnant with him when his father and his uncle, **Maffeo**, left their home in Venice, Italy, in 1253.

The Polos lived almost 800 years ago. In that era, many successful merchants traveled to other countries to buy and sell goods there. Those travels could be very dangerous. Merchants sometimes got caught in the middle of battles. They were attacked by bandits. They got sick. Traveling was a dirty, nasty business.

The two men traveled thousands of miles to China, then known as **Cathay**. The trip took years and it was almost impossible to send messages home. Marco may have thought his father and uncle were dead.

Niccolò and Maffeo Polo were very much alive. After being away for 16 years, they returned to Venice. Marco was not just glad to see his father. He wanted to hear his stories.

Niccolò talked about running the family business in **Constantinople** (now known as

*For pronunciations of words in **bold**, see page 47.

Istanbul, in modern-day Turkey). He described the difficult trip he'd taken through the Middle East. And he told his son about meeting **Kublai Khan**, who ruled over the greatest empire on earth.

When Niccolò and Maffeo left Venice again, Marco joined them. During the next quarter of a century, he would visit places few Europeans had ever seen. Unlike explorers hundreds of years later, Marco did not hope to discover new lands for his country. He wanted to be a merchant like his father. He dreamed of making money while learning all he could about different countries.

His travels did not make him famous. His book did.

Called *The Description of the World* (and also *The Travels of Marco Polo*), the book was exactly that. The description of the world. In the front of the book, Marco promised "a clear and ordered account, as told by the wise and noble Venetian Marco Polo, of the things he saw with his own eyes and of a few things which he did not see himself by which he was told by honest men."[1]

Marco described a world unknown to most Europeans. His book became a trusted guide. Christopher Columbus scribbled notes on its pages. Today, over 700 years after it was written, people can still use it to find the places Marco saw. But in the beginning, Marco Polo's horizons reached only to the edge of Venice, where he was a little boy growing up without a father.

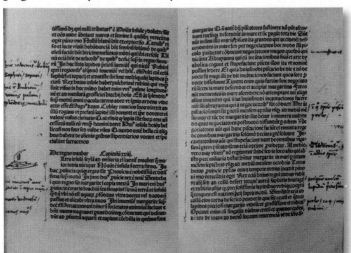

Marco Polo's *The Description of the World* with handwritten notes and sketches by Christopher Columbus

Marco Polo's book would be translated into English, German, and Latin, but at the time it was written, books could only be copied by hand onto parchment—the flat, stiff skin of an animal. This process took a long time and was costly. Most people who owned Marco Polo's book were scholars or members of the nobility.

Besides the expense, copying by hand made it easy for mistakes to happen. Even worse, some people who copied books added their own opinions or their own style. More than 100 copies of *The Description of the World* were produced between 1300 and 1500. No two of them are alike.

German printer **Johannes Gutenberg** made the production of books simple. In 1455, the Gutenberg Bible was printed. It changed the world of books forever. Now they could be produced in much larger quantities and for far less money. In 1477, the first printed version of *The Description of the World* was published. Now far more people could read about Marco Polo's adventures.

In 1847, this Lennox copy became the first Gutenberg Bible to reach the United States.

Armed with arrows and a sword, dressed as a Mongolian trader, Marco Polo became comfortable with the customs of the Mongols who ruled over China.

CHAPTER 2
Meeting the Great Khan

By the 1200s, Venice had become a powerful city-state. A community of over one hundred small islands nestled just off the **Adriatic** Sea, it was a gateway for merchants who wanted to buy and sell with Asian traders. Goods from Asia entering Venice were sold across Europe.

The Polo brothers were just two of many Venetian merchants trying to get rich buying and selling jewels and silks. In 1253, they boarded a ship for Constantinople. It was the center of European art and commerce.

By 1260, Constantinople had become a dangerous place. Merchants from Greece and Genoa fought with merchants from Venice for control of the city's markets. Marco wrote that, "with great prudence they [his father and uncle] decided, after some discussion, to cross the Black Sea with the intention of increasing their trade."[1]

On water and on land, merchants worried about thieves who might kill them for whatever they could steal. Hoping to stay safe, Niccolò and Maffeo dressed in old, filthy clothes. They sewed their jewels into the lining.

In this illustration from the *Book of the Wonders of the World,* the two Polo brothers are shown as they leave Constantinople.

At that time, there were no safe and easy ways to travel. While land travel could be dirty and dangerous, taking a ship was often worse. Boats were infested with rats and other vermin. They could be captured by dangerous pirates. Boats often sank during storms.

Crossing the Black Sea to **Sudak**, **Crimea**, the Polos hoped to sell their jewels. Sudak was a crossroads where merchants from Europe and Asia met and traded goods.

Although the Polo family had sold goods there before, Niccolò and Maffeo were unsuccessful this time. They left Sudak and eventually entered the region where present-day Iraq is located. It was ruled by Barka Khan, a grandson of the great Mongol leader Genghis Khan.

In the century before Marco Polo's birth, warring Mongol nomads in Asia fought for land. Genghis Khan brought them together. He led tens of thousands of Mongols who invaded countries across Asia, including China.

"Genghis Khan, seeing so many courageous men, equipped them with bows and other arms and set out to conquer new countries," Marco Polo wrote. "In a short time he had defeated more than eight provinces. He neither harmed [the people who lived there] nor ravaged [destroyed] their countries; he formed alliances with them . . . people were glad to follow him because he was just and good."[2]

Barka Khan welcomed the Polo brothers. For a year, they enjoyed his protection. Then their luck ended.

A war broke out between Barka and **Hülegü**, another grandson of Genghis Khan. The conflict prevented people from traveling freely because of the risk of being taken prisoner by one side or the other, or even being killed.

Niccolò and Maffeo Polo could not go back to Venice. They could only go forward. So they took the road east.

Traveling east, Niccolò and Maffeo saw very few Europeans. When they stopped in the Central Asian town of **Bukhara** (in modern-day **Uzbekistan**) they found a lively place filled with traders. Unfortunately, the local roads were overrun with warring tribes.

The Polos stayed in Bukhara for three years. The long stay changed their fortunes. They attracted attention because they looked different from the other merchants. Hülegü's ambassador passed through Bukhara on his way to Cathay. After meeting the Polos, he told them that Kublai Khan, who was yet another grandson of Genghis Khan, ruled there. Cathay once had been very dangerous. Kublai Khan made it safe. One reason for his success involved a bit of European technology. "Kublai's relatives ruled all the way to Eastern Europe

In Bukhara, Niccolò and Maffeo Polo are given the opportunity of a lifetime when they are invited to Cathay by Hülegü's representative.

and he had heard of great catapults the Christians had used during the Crusades,"[3] writes Carrie Gracie of BBC News. Marco later wrote that the ambassador said, "The Great Khan of the Tartars [Kublai Khan] has never seen a man of [Italian background] and he greatly wishes to meet one. Let me take you to him. I assure you that he will be very pleased to see you and will welcome you with all honor."[4] To sweeten his offer, the ambassador added that because of all the fighting outside Bukhara, the two men would be safer with him.

The Polos knew he was right. The trip would still be dangerous, but they could be the first merchants from Europe to visit Kublai Khan. If everything worked out, they could become very rich.

It took them a year to reach Kublai Khan. As Marco wrote, the Khan "was pleased to see them and made them very welcome."[5] He asked his visitors many questions—about their emperors, whether they ruled wisely, their wars, and so on.

More than anything else, Kublai Khan wanted to know about Christianity. Although a few European missionaries may have visited Cathay, he had a limited understanding of the religion. Kublai Khan was extremely tolerant. He allowed people in his kingdom to practice whatever religion they chose. Later, Marco Polo would notice the Khan holding a variety of different religious observances that included Jewish, Muslim, Christian, and Buddhist celebrations. He later told Marco, "I honor and respect all four and through them I honor Almighty God who is in heaven and to whom I pray for help."[6]

Kublai Khan wanted the Polos to go back to Europe and conduct a mission for him. They were to deliver a goodwill message to the Pope. Afterward, the brothers were to return to Cathay with 100 priests. The priests should be very wise, he explained, so they could prove their religion was the best. If he agreed, the Mongols would become Christians. Finally, he wanted the brothers to bring him oil from Jesus's grave.

The brothers knew if they made Kublai Khan happy they could become successful merchants in Cathay. They accepted the challenge.

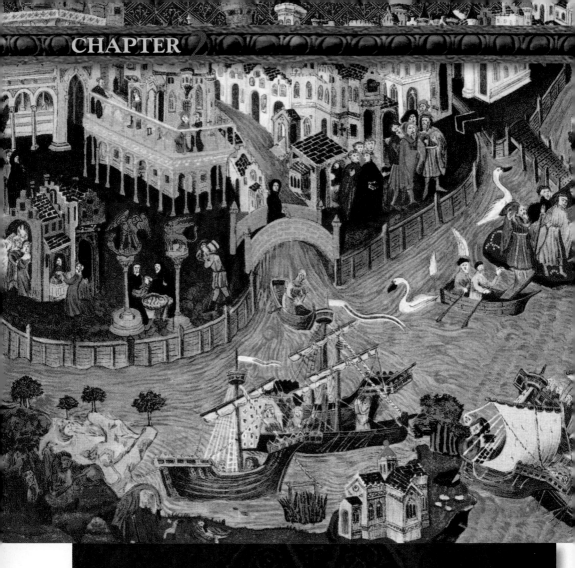

In this painting, the lower half depicts the Polos leaving Venice, while the many sights Marco will see are shown in the upper half.

The long journey home was just as difficult. When they reached the town of **Acre** (in modern-day Israel), they spoke to an important church official named **Teobaldo** of **Piacenza**. He told them the Pope had died. Until a new pope was elected, he could not help.

Niccolò and Maffeo did not want to wait. They went back to Venice. They had been gone for 16 years.

The Crusades

The Crusades were a series of wars launched over the city of Jerusalem. Christians saw Jerusalem as the place where Jesus Christ was crucified. Muslims viewed it as the place where Mohammed rose to heaven.

In 637, Arabs took control of Jerusalem. In 1095, they closed it to Christians. In response, the Pope asked for volunteers to join a crusade—an army that would retake the city. Over 30,000 men left Western Europe and captured the city in 1099. The Second Crusade, launched in 1147, sought to reinforce Jerusalem but accomplished little.

The Muslims retook Jerusalem in 1187. The Third Crusade set out right away but failed to dislodge the Muslims. The Fourth Crusade lasted from 1202 to 1204. Its focus was not Jerusalem but Constantinople. Crusaders burned libraries and stole money and jewelry they claimed would go toward the rescue of Jerusalem.

Perhaps the saddest Crusade was the Children's Crusade in 1212. Thousands of French and German children set off to reach the Holy City. Most died or quit before leaving Europe. The few who set sail drowned or were sold into slavery. The final Crusade began in 1291. It also failed and left Muslims in control of Jerusalem for centuries.

The Children's Crusade in 1212
by Gustave Doré (1832–1883)

As publishing became more modernized, books like *Marco Polo's Travels* became more widely read. Seen here is the frontispiece of a Nuremberg, Germany 1477 edition of the book.

CHAPTER 3
On the Road Again

Niccolò Polo stayed in Venice for two years. He remarried and had another child. Over two years after the Polo brothers had returned home, the church still had not selected a new Pope. Finally, Niccolò Polo decided he could no longer wait.

In 1271, he sailed to Acre. This time, Marco, now 17, joined Niccolò and Maffeo.

There still wasn't a new pope. Teobaldo gave them permission to visit Jesus's gravesite in Jerusalem and obtain the holy oil Kublai Khan had asked for.

They met again with Teobaldo in Acre. "We can see that the election of a new pope is being continually delayed," they explained. "We would like to return to the Great Khan for we are beginning to feel that we have waited too long."[1]

Since Teobaldo could not provide 100 priests, he gave them an official letter. It said they had done all they could do.

Bearing holy letters and holy oil, the travelers felt well-prepared for the Great Khan. Their trip ended suddenly at the Armenian port of **Layas**. As Marco remembered, "they learnt that the very

Hoping to fulfill the Kublai Khan's desire for 100 Christian priests, Niccolò and Maffeo Polo presented the Khan's letter to Teobaldo of Piacenza (later Pope Gregory X).

Teobaldo of Piacenza who had welcomed them had been elected . . . and had taken the name, 'Pope Gregory [X].' "[2]

The Polos returned to Acre and met with the new Pope. He told them he believed in their mission. He still could not spare 100 priests, but offered two friars who belonged to a religious order that pledged to never own anything. He also offered new letters he had written as the Pope to the Khan.

The Polo family felt protected from harm by Kublai Khan's gold tablets and the Pope's letters. The friars were less certain. As the group crossed into Armenia, the Sultan of Egypt invaded. Battles exploded across the land. The friars abandoned the mission, but the Polos continued.

They went north, passing Mount **Ararat**. According to legend, Noah's ark settled atop the mountain after the Great Flood. Marco didn't see any sign of the famous ship.

Although unable to bring 100 priests, in 1275 Niccolò and Maffeo Polo were able to offer Kublai Khan a letter and religious gifts from Pope Gregory X.

The Polos crossed into what is now Iraq. Of all the cities there, Marco would later describe **Tabriz** as the grandest. It was filled with beautiful gardens. Its people were prosperous and did a lively trade with merchants from the surrounding area. Most people were Muslims. He believed the religion let them "[harm] as they please men of other religions; they may assault and rob them . . . if not for the supervision and authority of the government they would do a great deal of evil."[3]

Marco and his family traveled in a large group of merchants called a caravan. There was usually safety in numbers. That changed as they crossed into Iran. A band of outlaws called the Karaunas attacked. Local legend claimed they could turn the day into night and use the darkness to rob and kidnap travelers. Marco claimed to have survived this magic, managing to escape along with his father and uncle. But

Marco Polo in later life

The years-long trip from Venice to Cathay was filled with adventure, new sights and the ever-present threat of death. The three Polos crossed deserts and mountain ranges, battling disease and the elements in hopes of becoming rich from Asian silks and treasures.

he noted that many people they had been traveling with "were caught, however, and were sold as slaves; and some were even killed."[4]

After that adventure, the Polos were happy to reach the port of **Hormuz**. Sea travel was the fastest way to reach China. They quickly changed their minds when they saw the ships they would be sailing on. Marco claimed they often sank because "instead of being nailed together with iron nails, the planks are sewn together with thread made from coconut husks."[5]

They turned around and continued their trip on land. Their progress was stopped when Marco became sick shortly after entering Afghanistan. It was a year before he was well enough to travel.

Marco would need all his strength because the **Pamir** Mountains lay ahead. It grew so cold that they no longer saw birds. It was very hard to cook food because of the lack of oxygen at such a high elevation. They needed well over a month to reach the other side.

They traded mountains for a flat landscape that was even deadlier. Between the Polos and Cathay lay hundreds of miles of desert. The dry land was broken only occasionally by oasis towns like **Khotan**, with green landscapes and plenty of water and food. Then they entered **Taklimakan**—the "Desert of Death."

After surviving Takilmakan, the three arrived in the city of Lop before undertaking the most difficult part of the journey: the Gobi Desert. "Travelers preparing to cross the Great [Gobi] Desert," Marco wrote, "with their camels rest in this city for a week before beginning their journey. It is said it would take a year to cross the whole desert and a month in the narrowest parts."[6]

The Gobi seemed endless. During the day, the temperature reached 100 degrees and even higher. At night, it dropped below freezing. They relied on whatever food and water they packed. The water they found was too dangerous to drink.

In 1275, nearly four years after leaving Venice, the Polos reached the court of Kublai Khan.

According to the Bible, Noah escaped the Great Flood by building a giant ark or boat. He took two of every kind of animal on board with him. Finally the flood waters receded, and "on the seventeenth day of the seventh month the ark came to rest on the Mountains of Ararat." (Genesis 8:4, New International Version Bible).

"Noah's Ark," an 1846 painting by Edward Hicks (1780–1849)

The highest mountain in modern-day Turkey, Mount Ararat has two peaks. Greater Ararat is 16,854 feet (5,137 meters) high, while Lesser Ararat is 12,782 feet (3,896 meters) and runs along the country's eastern border with Iran.

For centuries, the faithful have sought evidence that Noah's Ark really did settle atop Mount Ararat. In March 2006, researchers uncovered a rock formation resembling a huge ice-covered ark. In February 2011, a group of Chinese and Turkish explorers claimed to have found the ark's wooden remains. They claimed that scientific tests proved it was 4,800 years old, the time when Christians believe Noah's ark floated atop the waters of the Great Flood. But thus far nothing has been proven conclusively.

The structure claimed to be Noah's Ark near Mount Ararat in Agri, Turkey.

In 2006, it was revealed as a rock formation, a naturally occurring phenomena.

Barely an adult, Marco Polo must have felt overwhelmed and excited by Beijing when he reached it after a long and dangerous trip. This painting by American artist James McConnell (1907–1998) reveals the vast differences in clothing and lifestyle between Europeans and the residents of Cathay.

CHAPTER 4
Representing the Khan

Kublai Khan was in his summer castle at **Xanadu**, about 200 miles (320 kilometers) north of Beijing. Though the Polos did not bring any of the priests the Khan had requested, he was pleased with the oil which he believed had magical healing powers. Still, he was less interested in gifts than in the young man who arrived with Niccolò and Maffeo. During the journey, Marco had studied the Mongol language. Soon after his arrival, he learned several more languages. That made it easier to communicate during his stay.

Marco was impressed by the Khan's summer court. He was overwhelmed by the ruler's winter palace in Beijing. The Khan often held banquets which served up to 40,000 diners. When Niccolò and Maffeo left for long trading trips, the Khan became like a father to Marco. He took him on hunting trips, in which the Mongol leader used a trained cheetah. He shared his love of falconry, a sport enjoyed by Europeans as well as Mongolians. All these activities helped Marco gain the Khan's trust. Then the Khan did something extraordinary. He made Marco Polo his personal ambassador to

This miniature from *Livre des merveilles du monde*, or the *Book of the Wonders of the World*, shows Kublai Khan hunting with a cheetah. During his reign, lions and other wild cats were used to help catch prey.

southwest China. Traveling there, Marco passed Tibet and became the first European to write about that small country. He described a place destroyed by Mongu Khan (another grandson of Genghis Khan). "For twenty days the traveler must pass through uninhabited villages where roaming lions, bears and lynxes make the journey very dangerous," he wrote. "Merchants traveling through these regions use very large canes growing here to defend themselves."[1] He also wrote about Burma and the east coast of Africa, although he almost certainly didn't visit those places.

Decades later, many people would ask to hear about Marco's explorations. He told very interesting stories about the places he visited. He had developed those skills in Beijing. He learned by listening to others who returned from travels for the Khan. The Khan was often unhappy with them, calling them "foolish and ignorant if they could tell him nothing about the countries they had visited, because in fact he was more interested in the customs of those countries than the missions,"[2] Marco wrote.

The Khan never regarded Marco as "foolish and ignorant." No matter where he journeyed, Marco always paid careful attention to his surroundings and the people he met. That way he could deliver interesting reports to the Khan. Marco also "collected for himself many unusual objects,"[3] due to his own curiosity and his training as a merchant.

Because he did such a good job, the Khan made Marco Polo governor of **Yangchow** for three years. During that time, he visited **Quinsai** (today known as **Hangzhou**). He called it the "city of heaven." With over one million people living in a city one hundred miles around, it was unlike any he had ever seen. It may have been the largest city in the world at the time.

In 1284, Marco Polo left China on an official visit to India. He also spent time in the Kingdom of **Champa**—a large country where **Sumatra**, Malaya, Thailand and Vietnam are today.

Many of his trips for Kublai Khan took place because of the leader's interest in the world's religions. South of India, in Sri Lanka, Marco bought a relic—a very old religious item. The sellers claimed it was Buddha's tooth. The Khan paid a great deal of money for it.

Along the Indian Coast, Marco described seeing yogis. These Hindu masters went days without food. They spent their lives naked, sleeping at night on hard ground without a mattress or a blanket.

Along with descriptions of travel that are still used by modern day explorers, Marco Polo also offered fantastic stories about incredible creatures like these men with heads like dogs as seen in this miniature from *Livre des merveilles du monde* or the *Book of the Wonders of the World.*

Relying on the descriptions of others, along with his own experiences, Marco Polo described mythical creatures as well as real ones like these dragons, griffins and other fantastic animals as seen in a miniature from *Livre des merveilles du monde*, or the *Book of the Wonders of the World*.

Eventually all three Polos were back in Beijing. Niccolò and Maffeo were growing old and tired. Their trade in Cathay had made them very rich, but they missed Venice. They were also worried that since Kublai Khan was well into his 70s, he could die at any time. If that happened, people who were jealous of their influence with the ruler could put their lives in danger. They begged the Kublai Khan to let them go home. He refused.

The Silk Road

During their travels, the Polos often made use of a network of trade routes known as the Silk Road, which had been developed centuries before Marco Polo was born. For European merchants, the Silk Road was the fastest path to Asian customers. This trade began with a tiny moth called a silkworm. As a caterpillar, it produces hundreds of feet of silk from its salivary glands. This creates a cocoon.

To make silk cloth, the cocoons are boiled in water for five minutes. Afterward, the silk is unraveled into thread which is put on a loom. The loom is used to weave the thread into cloth. The cocoons of 3,000 silkworms produce enough thread for 2.2 pounds (or one kilogram) of silk cloth.

European's desire for silk clothing fed the trade with the Chinese, who kept the process of silk production a secret. Under Kublai Khan's rule, the Silk Road became so safe that one traveler claimed "a young woman would have been able to travel with a golden tray on her head with no fear."[4]

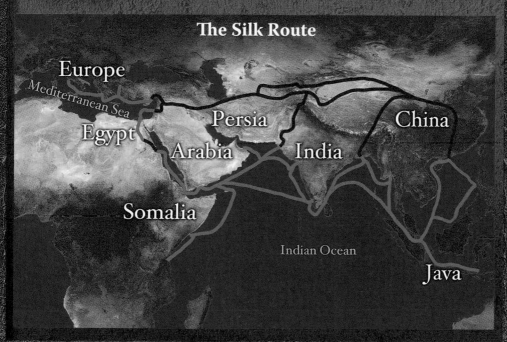

The Silk Route

Europe

Mediterranean Sea

Egypt

Persia

Arabia

India

China

Somalia

Indian Ocean

Java

If Marco Polo hadn't been captured in Genoa and thrown in jail, he never would have met fellow prisoner Rustichello da Pisa, and he wouldn't have co-authored one of the world's most famous travel books—*The Description of the World (The Travels of Marco Polo)*.

CHAPTER 5
Returning Home

Their ticket home came when ambassadors for the Khan's newly widowed grand-nephew, **Arghun Khan**, arrived at the Khan's court in 1292. They wanted to bring a bride back to Persia for Arghun Khan to marry. Kublai Khan offered them a 17-year-old princess. Because Marco had acquired a lot of seagoing experience, the ambassadors asked him to escort the princess on the long voyage. "The Great Khan loved the Polo family," Marco wrote, "and so it was only with reluctance that he allowed them to accompany the three barons and the lady."[1]

The Polo family boarded one of 14 ships, joining 600 other passengers and crew members. When the Polos reached Hormuz after a long voyage, there were only 18 survivors. The rest had died. While waiting for his new bride, Arghun Khan had died as well. The princess married his son. There had also been a much more momentous death: Kublai Khan.

Now there was no reason for the Polos to return to Cathay. They sailed for Venice, where they arrived in 1295.

Exhaustive in its details and descriptions, *The Description of the World (The Travels of Marco Polo)* was widely read (and doubted) during the last years of Polo's life.

Marco had been in China for 17 years, and in all the Polos had been gone for 24 years. When they arrived in Venice, their family did not recognize them. With their faded, dirty clothes and scruffy appearance, the Polos did not look like rich merchants.

Eventually, they convinced their family that they were indeed Niccolò, Maffeo and Marco Polo. Once their family believed them, they performed a great trick. Cutting into their clothes, they released a slew of jewels. Diamonds, emeralds and rubies clattered onto the floor.

Marco joined the family business. He settled into the life of a Venetian merchant, sharing stories about his adventures with anyone who listened. When Venice got into a war with nearby Genoa in 1298, Marco commanded a ship, crew and soldiers he paid for. Unfortunately, he was captured and thrown in jail.

Prison life wasn't too harsh. Marco had good meals. But he was bored. He passed the time describing his adventures. One of his listeners was a famous writer named Rustichello da Pisa, who'd also fought against Genoa. He asked Marco to let him write down the stories. Marco agreed.

Marco Polo was released from prison in August 1299. The book was published as *The Description of the World*. As a merchant he had a good eye for details which helped the book become very popular.

Marco grew old in Venice. Shortly after his release from the Genoese prison, he married a woman named **Donata Badoer**. They had three daughters, **Fantina**, **Bellela**, and **Moretta**. He continued to be successful as a merchant, but many knew him for his book. He carried a copy everywhere he went.

However, some people thought he had made up the stories. As Marco lay dying late in 1323, a priest named **Jacopo d'Acqui** visited his bedside. He had read *The Description of the World*, and as he later recalled, because the book contained so many "almost unbelievable things [Marco] was [asked] by his friends when he was at the point of death to correct his book and [take back] those things that he had

A writer of romance novels, Rustichello da Pisa caught a big break when Marco Polo arrived and began to tell him the stories of his adventures, as he does here in their Genoa prison cell.

written over and above the truth. To which he replied, 'Friends, I have not written down the half of those things that I saw.' "[2]

Marco Polo died early the next year, on the evening between January 8 and 9th. In 1995, Frances Wood's book *Did Marco Go to China?* tried to prove what the priest and many Venetians suspected. It laid out evidence that Marco had never visited the places he wrote about. Wood claimed the traveler never got further than Crimea. In support of this idea, he noted that Marco never mentioned common Chinese practices such as binding the feet of young girls or the famous Great Wall of China.

National Geographic writer Michael Yamashita set out to prove Wood wrong by using *The Travels of Marco Polo* as a guide. Marco wrote before GPS devices or even decent maps, yet **Yamashita** says, "we were constantly amazed at how accurate a reporter Marco was . . . In Iran, he led us to the same hot spring he had written about." Marco Polo described places so exactly, the writer believed he had to have visited them. "With each triumphant find, I became more and more convinced that Marco had to have been writing from firsthand experience,"[3] he wrote.

Because Marco was the emperor's guest, he probably did not see many practices of common people. The Great Wall of China was built hundreds of years after Marco visited. For many people who have traveled in his footsteps, and those who have read the story of his journey, Marco Polo's world is very real.

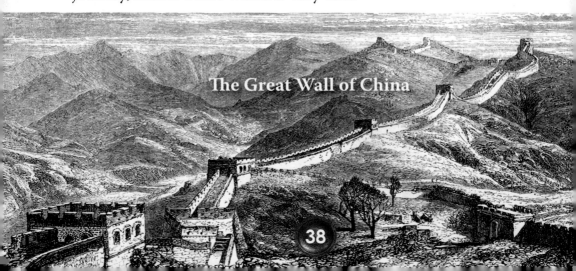
The Great Wall of China

The first time many children hear the name Marco Polo comes when they play a game in a swimming pool. The game is easy. The person who is "it" closes their eyes and says the name "Marco." Everyone else responds by saying "Polo." This process continues as the person who is "it" tries to tap one of the other players. If they succeed, then that person is it.

But why is a game about being lost named after the great traveler? Some people suggest it is because the Polo family took so long to reach China and traveled a route which was neither direct nor straight.

Another explanation lies with Marco's description of the Great Desert outside of Lop. He said travelers in groups often fell asleep on their camels at night. When they woke up, sometimes no one was around. They could hear voices of other people in their groups calling their name and wandering aimlessly. According to Marco, travelers hung bells around their animals' necks so others could hear them.

Marco Polo's Caravan

Compendious Map of Marco Polo's Asia
and adjacent countries

Conjectural route of the elder Polos   Conjectural route of Marco Polo

Traveling on camel, by ship and on foot, Marco Polo, along with his father Niccolò and his uncle Maffeo crossed Asia. The trip was thousands of miles long and took several years to complete. The return voyage was even more hazardous.

Statue of Marco Polo in Hangzhou, China, near the West Lake

1253	Niccolò Polo, Marco's father, and Marco's uncle, Maffeo Polo, leave Venice.
1254	Marco Polo is born in Venice, Italy.
1269	Niccolò and Maffeo return to Venice; Marco's mother dies while the two brothers are away.
1271	Marco leaves Venice with his father and his uncle.
1274	The three Polos reach China.
1275–1292	Marco Polo serves at the court of Kublai Khan and travels extensively through China as the Khan's personal ambassador, making careful notes of everything he sees.
1292	The Polos leave China.
1295	The Polos arrive home in Venice.
1298	Marco commands a galley in a war between Venice and Genoa; he is captured and put in jail, where he tells his story to his cellmate Rustichello da Pisa.
1299	Marco is freed and returns home to Venice.
1300	Marco marries Donata Badoer; they eventually have three daughters.
1324	Marco Polo dies in Venice, Italy.

1095	Christians launch the First Crusade to take Jerusalem from the Muslims.
1115	The Jin Dynasty is founded in Northern China.
1162	Genghis Khan is born in Mongolia.
1174	In England, fire ravages the Canterbury Cathedral.
1190	After being crowned King of England, Richard I leaves the country to join the Third Crusade.
1212	The Children's Crusade leads to the deaths of thousands of young French and Germans.
1215	The Magna Carta is signed at Runnymede, England; it is the first document limiting royal power.
1227	Genghis Khan dies.
1260	Kublai Khan is elected Great Khan by vote of Mongol armies.
1267	Kublai Khan moves the capital of China to Beijing.
1290	King Edward I signs a law forcing all Jewish people to leave England.
1294	Kublai Khan dies.
1337	England and France begin fighting in The Hundred Years War.
1347	The first people die from a plague called The Black Death; between 25–50 percent of Europe's population will die from the disease.
1440	Johannes Gutenberg invents moveable type.

Chapter 1: *A Description of the World*
1. Maria Bellonci, *The Travels of Marco Polo*, translated by Teresa Waugh (New York: Facts on File, 1984), p. 9.

Chapter 2: Meeting the Great Khan
1. Maria Bellonci, *The Travels of Marco Polo*, translated by Teresa Waugh (New York: Facts on File, 1984), p. 10.
2. Ibid., p. 69.
3. Carrie Gracie, "Kublai Khan: China's Favorite Barbarian," BBC News, October 8, 2012. http://www.bbc.co.uk/news/magazine-19850234
4. Bellonci, *Travels of Marco Polo*, p. 11.
5. Ibid., pp. 11–12.
6. Ibid., p. 69.

Chapter 3: On the Road Again
1. Maria Bellonci, *The Travels of Marco Polo*, translated by Teresa Waugh (New York: Facts on File, 1984), p. 14.
2. Ibid.
3. Ibid., pp. 28–29.
4. Ibid., p. 34.
5. Ibid.
6. Ibid., p. 46.

Chapter 4: Representing the Great Khan
1. Maria Bellonci, *The Travels of Marco Polo*, translated by Teresa Waugh (New York: Facts on File, 1984), p. 14.
2. Ibid., p. 17.
3. Ibid.
4. Laurence Bergreen, *Marco Polo: From Venice to Xanadu* (New York: Alfred A. Knopf, 2007), pp. 27–28.

Chapter 5: Returning Home
1. Maria Bellonci, *The Travels of Marco Polo*, translated by Teresa Waugh (New York: Facts on File, 1984), p. 19.
2. Laurence Bergreen, *Marco Polo: From Venice to Xanadu* (New York: Alfred A. Knopf, 2007), p. 339.
3. Michael Yamashita, *Marco Polo: A Photographer's Journey* (Vercelli, Italy: White Star, 201, pp. 11–12.

Books

Bandon, Alex and Patrick Brien. *The Travels of Marco Polo*. Austin, Texas: Steadwell Books, 2000.

Burgan, Michael. *Marco Polo: Marco Polo and the Silk Road to China*. Minneapolis, Minnesota: Compass Point Books, 2002.

Demi. *Marco Polo*. New York: Marshall Cavendish Children, 2008.

Freedman, Russell. *The Adventures of Marco Polo*. New York: Arthur A. Levine Books, 2006.

Markle, Sandra. *Animals Marco Polo Saw*. San Francisco, California: Chronicle Books, 2009.

McCarty, Nick. *Marco Polo: The Boy Who Traveled the Medieval World*. Washington, D.C.: National Geographic, 2006.

Ross, Stewart, and Stephen Biesty. *Into the Unknown: How Great Explorers Found Their Way by Land, Sea, and Air*. Somerville, Massachusetts: Candlewick Press, 2011.

On the Internet

Kids Biography—Marco Polo
http://www.silk-road.com/artl/marcopolo.shtml

Marco Polo—Kids Discover Magazine
http://www.kidsdiscover.com/marco-polo-for-kids

The Middle Ages for Kids: The Crusades
http://medievaleurope.mrdonn.org/crusades.html

Marco Polo (ca. 1254–1324), BBC History
http://www.bbc.co.uk/history/historic_figures/polo_marco.shtml

Marco Po lo for Kids
http://www.janisherbertforkids.com/html/marco_polo.html

Works Consulted

Belliveau, Denis, and Francis Donnell. *In the Footsteps of Marco Polo*. Lanham, Maryland: Rowman & Littlefield Publishers, 2008.

Bellonci, Maria. *The Travels of Marco Polo*. Translated by Teresa Waugh. New York: Facts on File, 1984.

Bergreen, Laurence. *Marco Polo: From Venice to Xanadu*. New York: Alfred A. Knopf, 2007.

Great Empires: An Illustrated Atlas. Washington, D.C.: National Geographic, 2012.

Yamashita, Michael. *Marco Polo: A Photographer's Journey*. Vercelli, Italy: White Star, 2002, 2011.

Periodicals

Gracie, Carrie. "Kublai Khan: China's Favorite Barbarian." *BBC News*, October 8, 2012. http://www.bbc.co.uk/news/magazine-19850234

"Marco Polo Never Traveled to the Far East," *Daily Mail* [London, England]. August 10, 2011. http://www.dailymail.co.uk/news/article-2024221/Marco-Polo-reached-China-picked-tales-Orient-Italians-claim.html

"Noah's Ark Found in Turkey," *The [London] Sun*. February 22, 2011. http://www.thesun.co.uk/sol/homepage/news/2949640/Noahs-Ark-found-in-Turkey.html?OTC-RSS&ATTR=News#ixzz0mIvTDKNW

Radford, Benjamin. "Baywatch Star the Latest to Abandon Search for Noah's Ark," Science on NBC News. August 22, 2012. http://www.msnbc.msn.com/id/48743600/ns/technology_and_science-science/t/baywatch-star-latest-abandon-search-noahs-ark/#.UNLqDo7TJHg

Ventimiglia (ven-tee-MEE-lee-uh)
Niccolò (nee-koh-LOH)
Maffeo (mah-FAY-oh)
Cathay (ka-THEY)
Constantinople
  (kon-stan-tih-NOH-puhl)
Istanbul (is-tahn-BOOL)
Kublai Khan (KOO-blahy KAHN)
Johannes Gutenberg (yoh-HAHN-
  uhs GOOT-n-burg)
Adriatic (ey-dree-AT-ik)
Sudak (soo-DAHK)
Crimea (krahy-MEE-uh)
Hülegü (hoo-LAY-goo)
Bukhara (boo-KAHR-uh)
Uzbekistan (ooz-BEK-uh-stan)
Acre (AH-kruh)
Teobaldo (tay-oh-BAL-doh)
Piacenza (pyah-CHEN-tsah)
Gustave Doré (goo-STAV
  daw-REY)
Nuremberg (NOOR-uhm-burg)
Layas (lie-AHS)
Ararat (AR-uh-rat)

Tabriz (tah-BREEZ)
Hormuz (hawr-MOOZ)
Pamir (pah-MEER)
Khotan (khoh-TAHN)
Taklimakan (tah-kluh-muh-KAHN)
Beiing (bey-JING)
Xanadu (ZAN-uh-doo)
Yangchow (yahng-CHOH)
Quinsai (keen-SIGH)
Hangzhou (hahng-JOH)
Champa (KAHM-pah)
Sumatra (soo-MAH-truh)
Genoa (JEN-oh-uh)
Rustichello da Pisa (roos-tee-KEL-
  loh da PEE-sah)
Arghun Khan (ar-GOON KAHN)
Donata Badoer (doh-NAH-tah
  bah-doh-AIR)
Fantina (fan-TEE-nah)
Moretta (mor-EHT-ah)
Jacopo d'Acqui (YAH-coh-poh
  dah-KWEE)
Yamashita (YAH-mah-SHEE-tah)

GLOSSARY

ambassador (am-BASS-uh-dohr)—The official representative of one
  country to another.
city-state (CIH-tee STATE)—Small independent area that is
  self-ruled.
empire (EHM-pyre)—Group of countries with one ruler, often
  assembled as a result of victories in battle.
Khan (KAWN)—Mongol name for ruler or leader.
merchant (MUHR-chunt)—Trader who makes money by buying or
  selling goods.
nomads (NOE-mads)—People who wander from place to place
  searching for food and water for themselves and for their
  animals.
prudence (PROO-dense)—Good judgment.
relic (REHL-ick)—An ancient object, often with religious importance.
vermin (VUHR-muhn)—Small animals and insects like rats, lice and
  fleas that can spread disease.

47